LOTS OF FISH

by Marileta Robinson

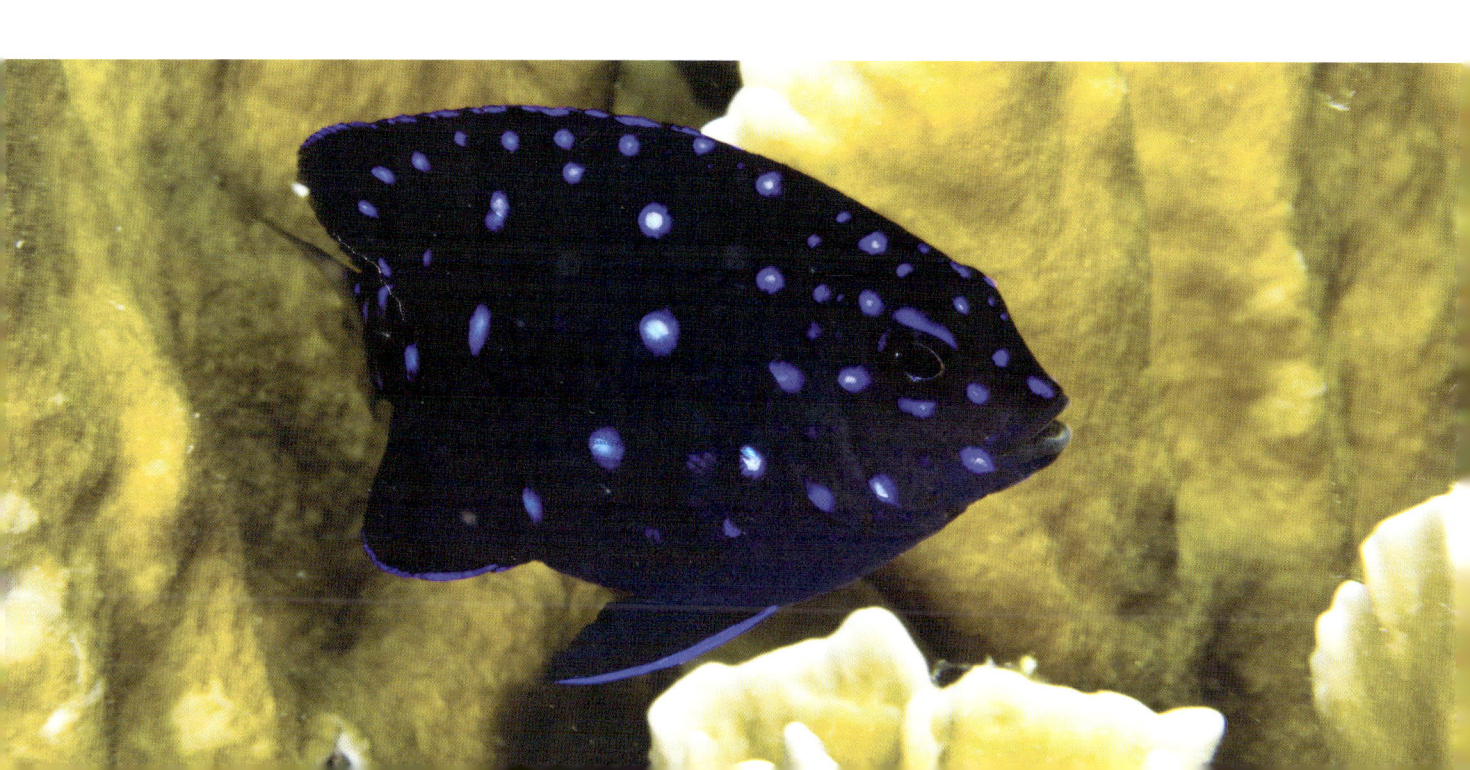

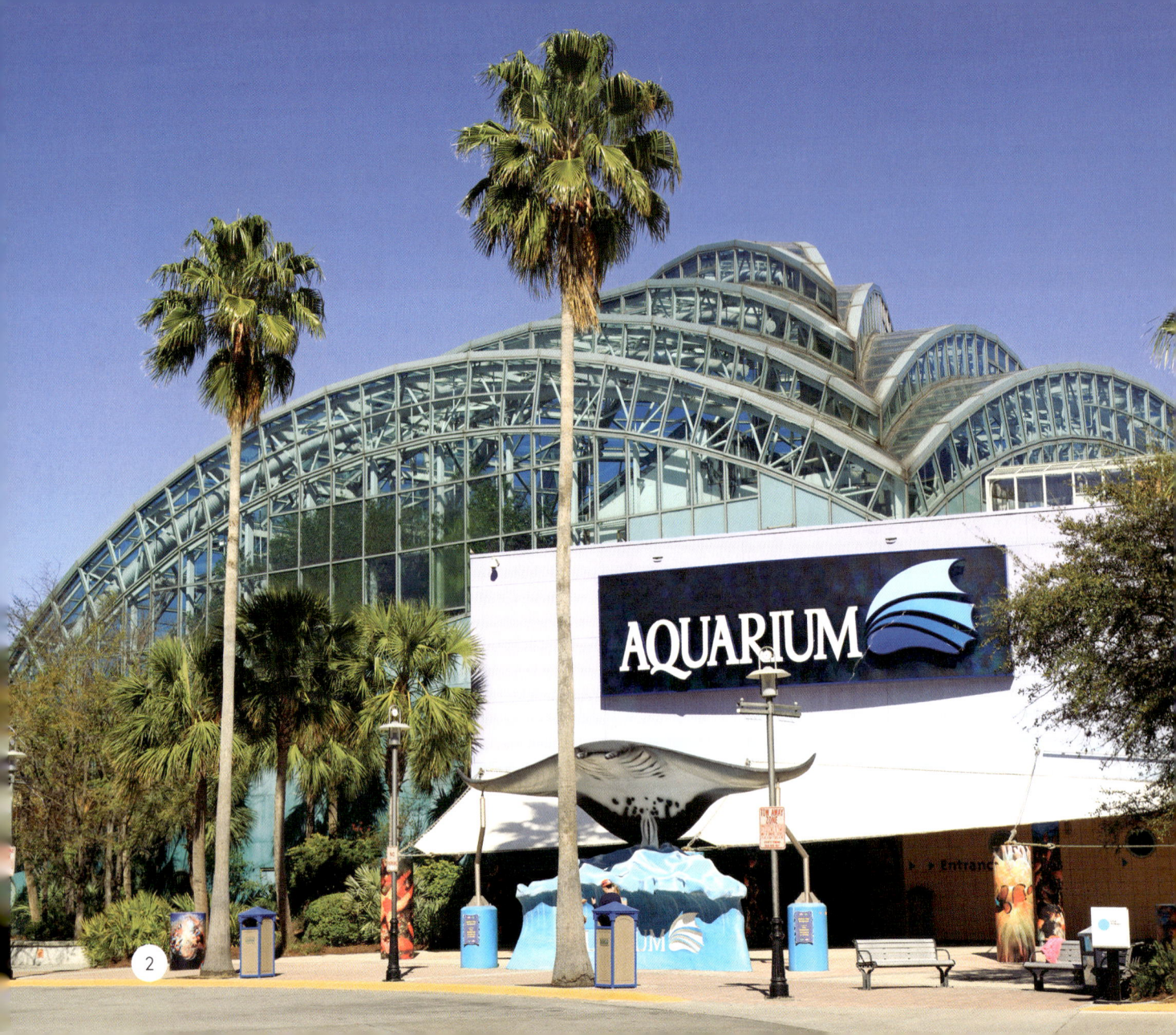

You come to see fish here.

You see little fish.

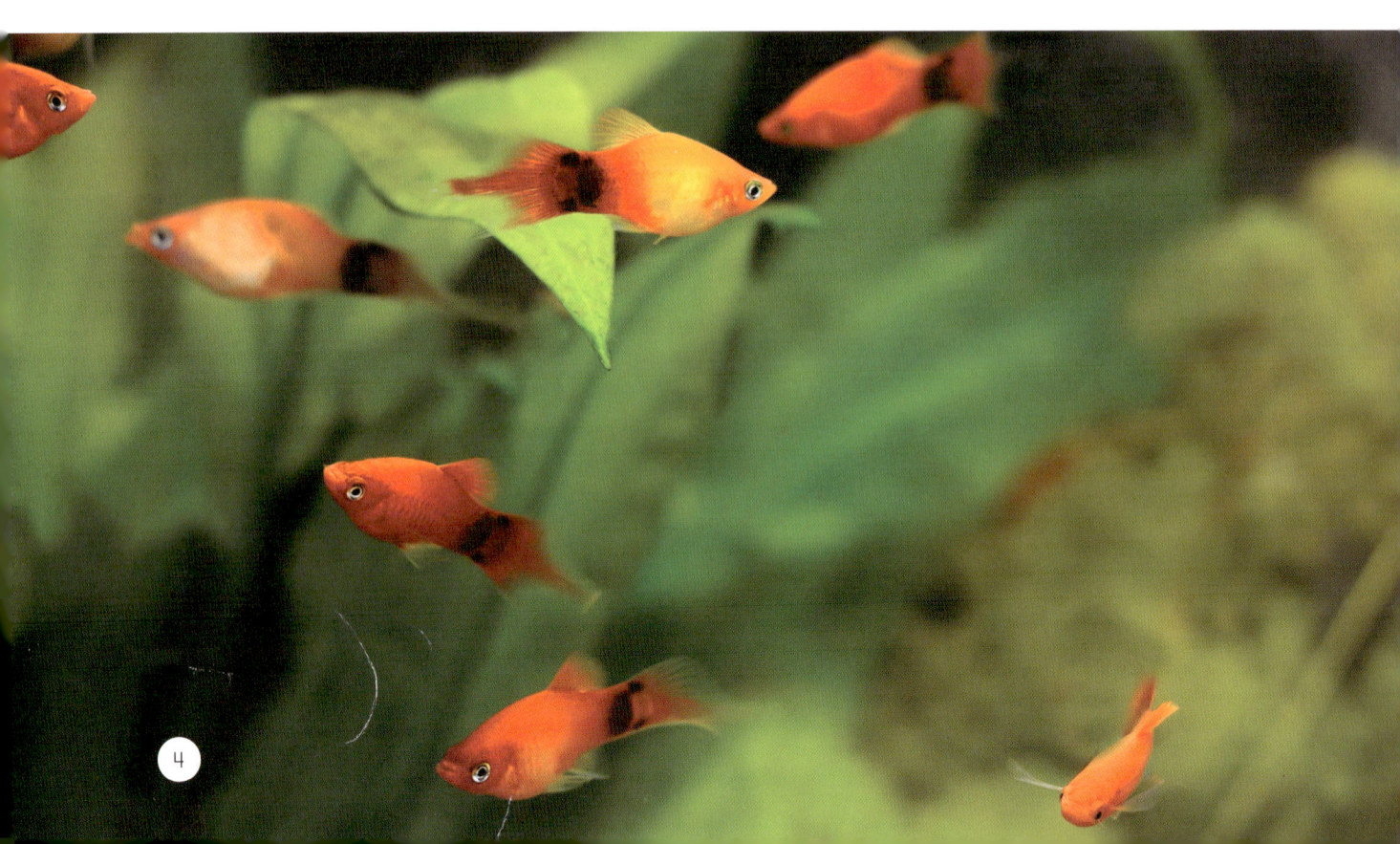

You see big fish.

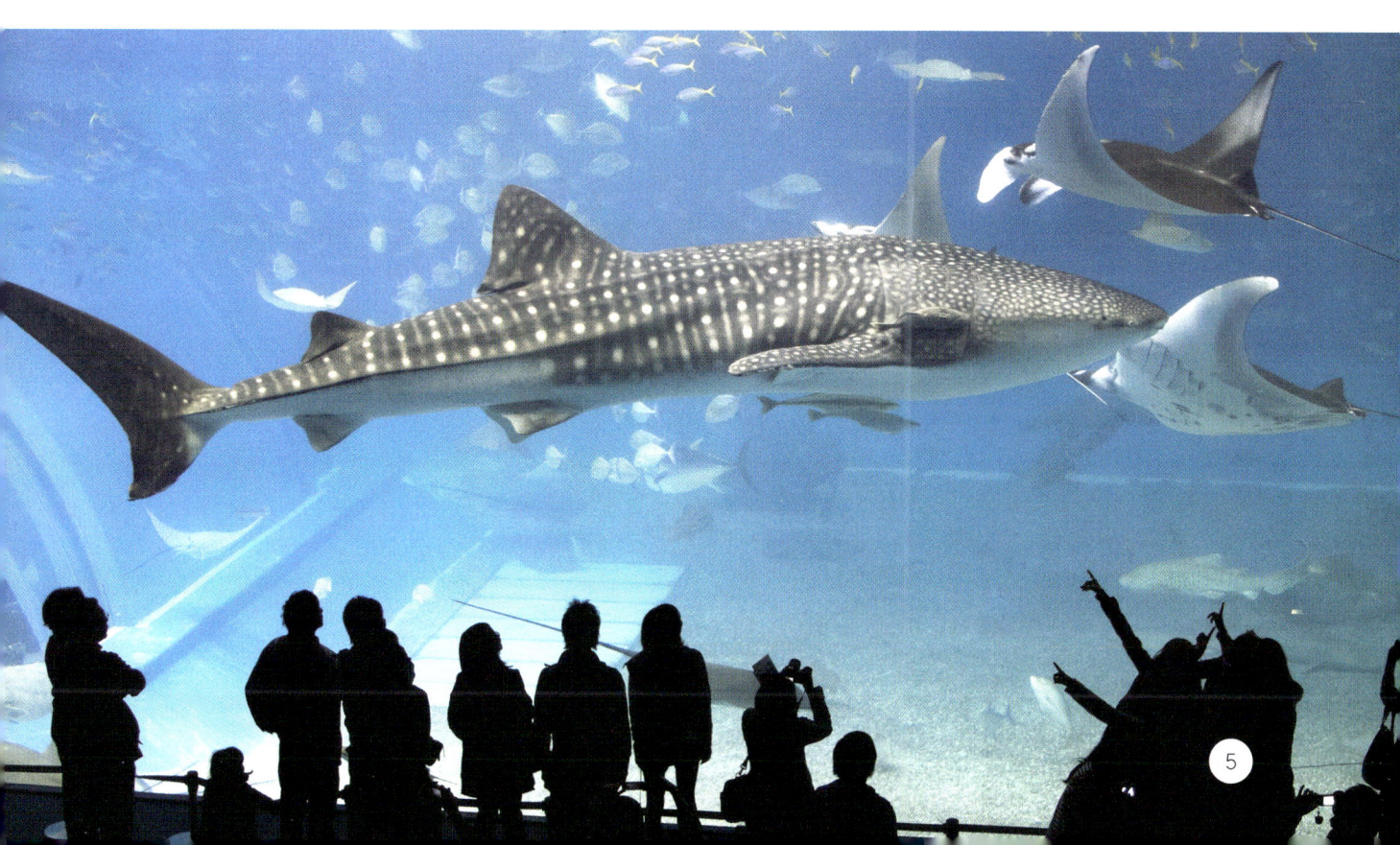

You see fat fish.

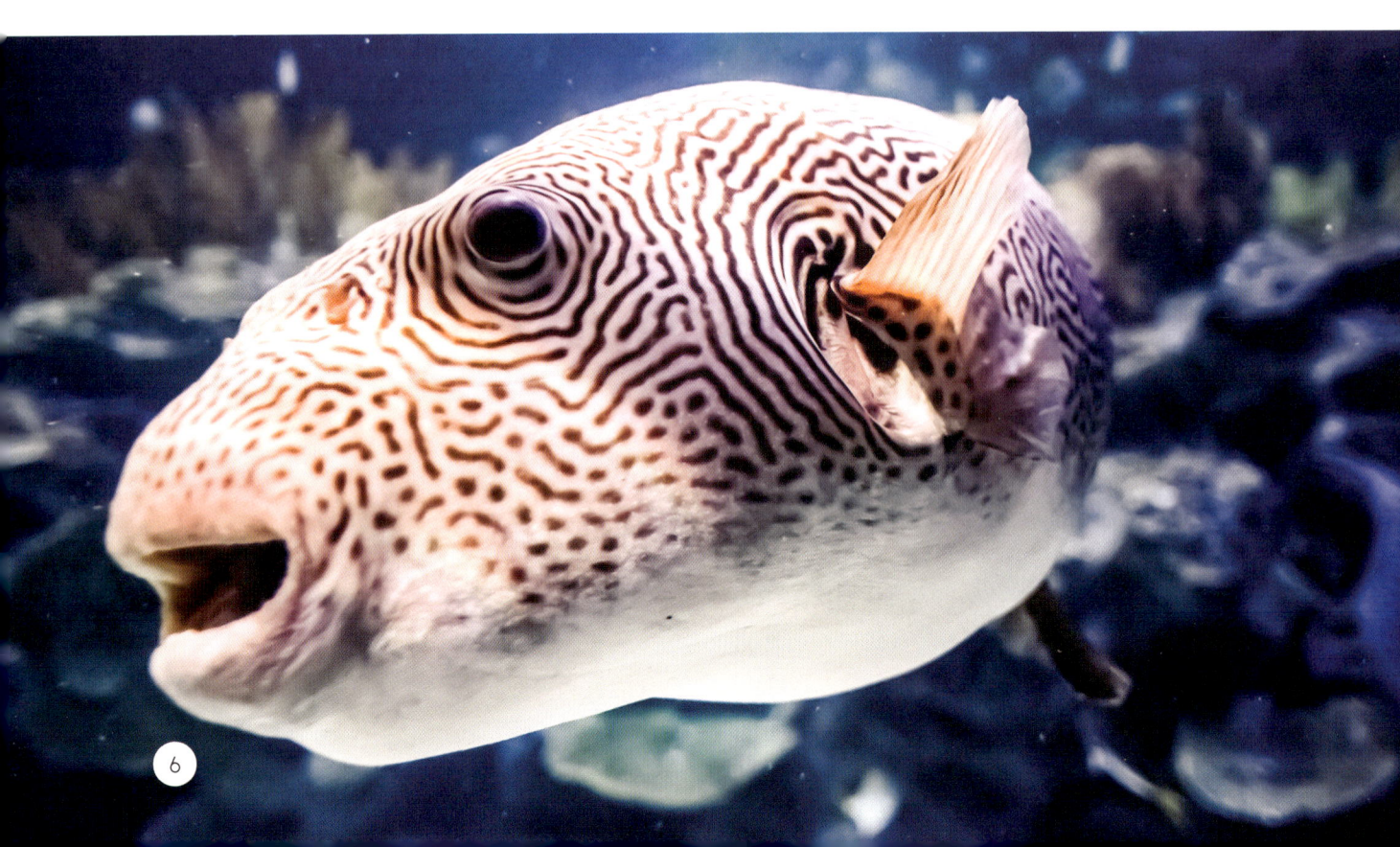

You see blue fish.

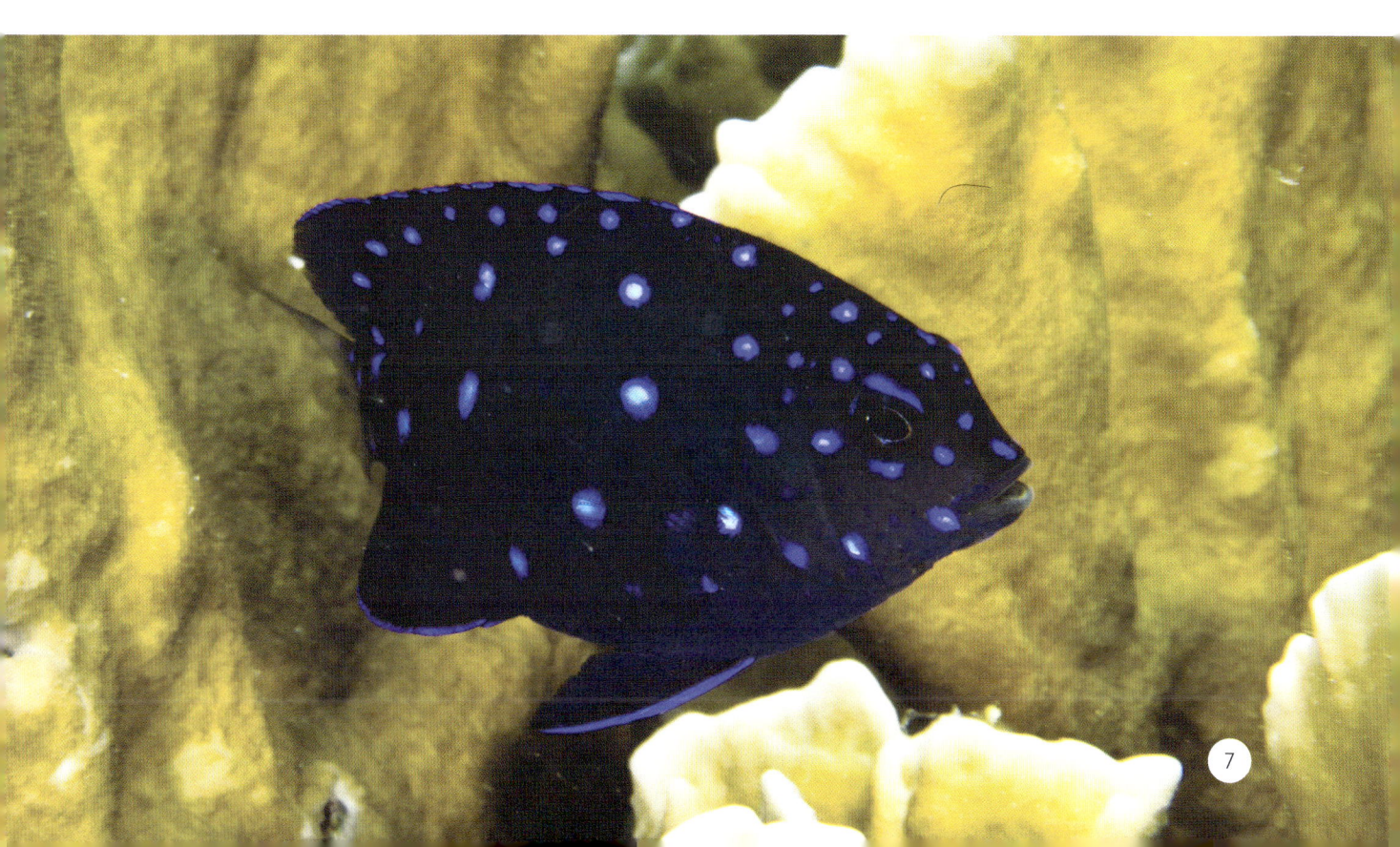

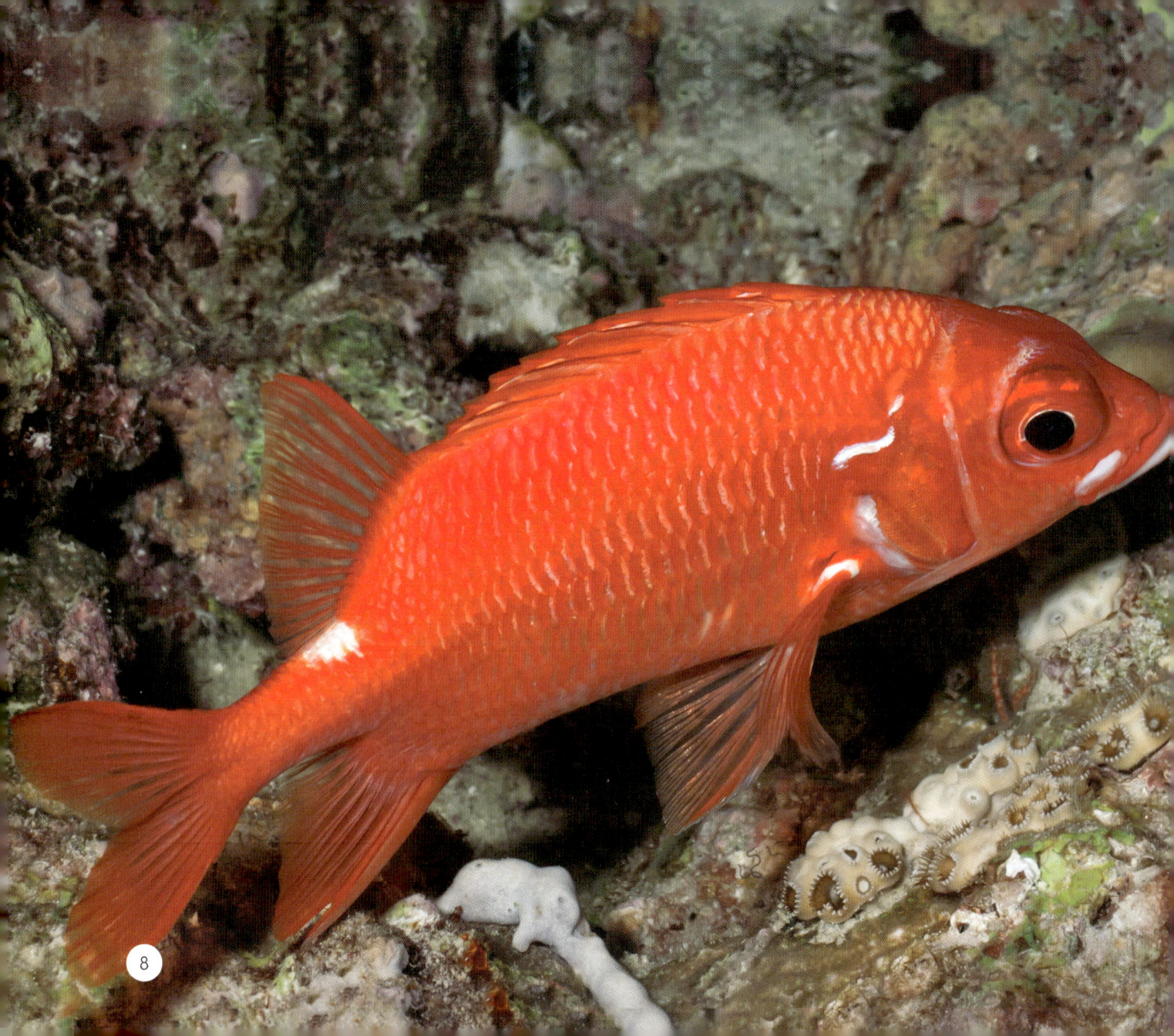

You see red fish.

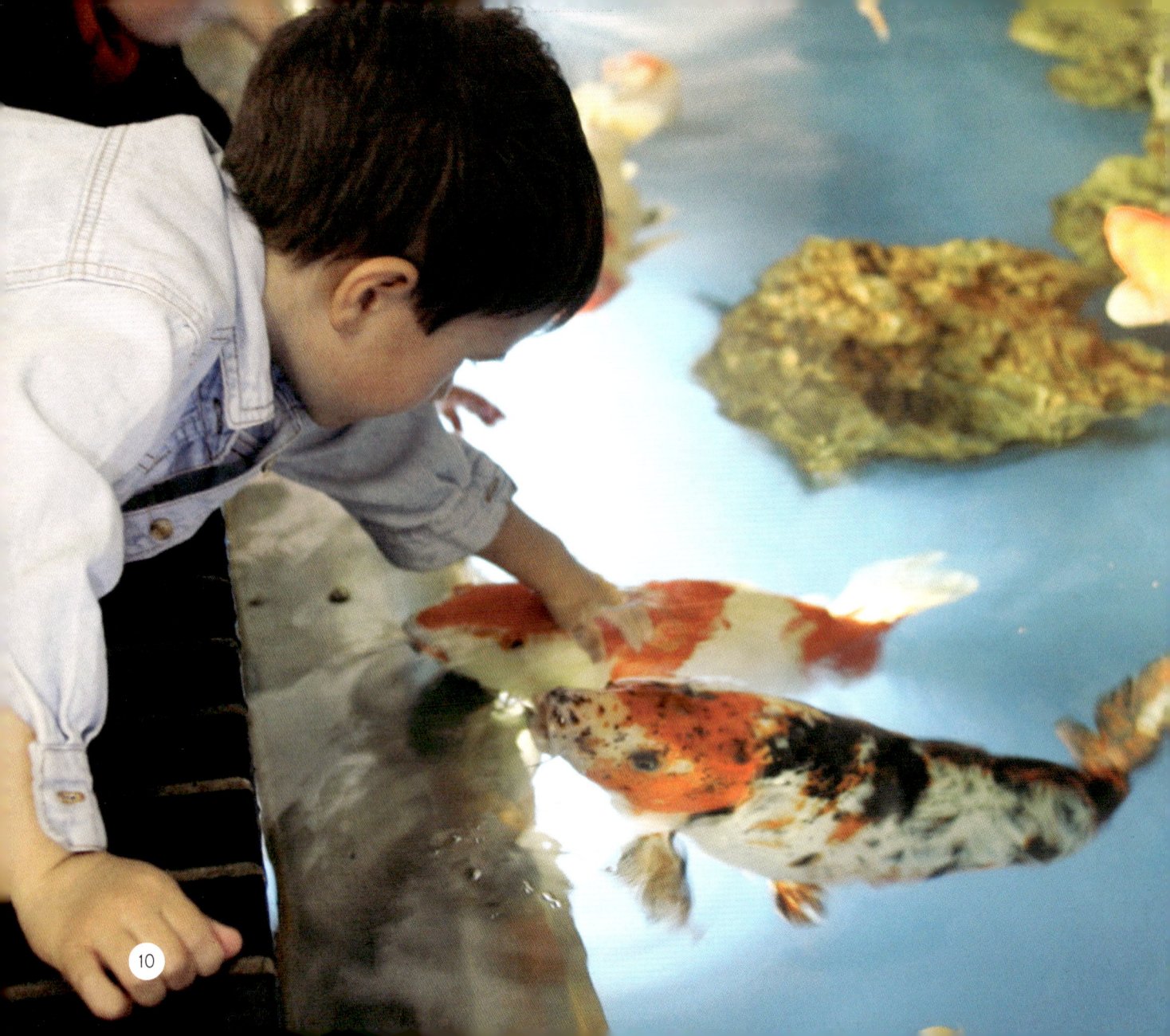

You pet a fish.

You feed a fish.

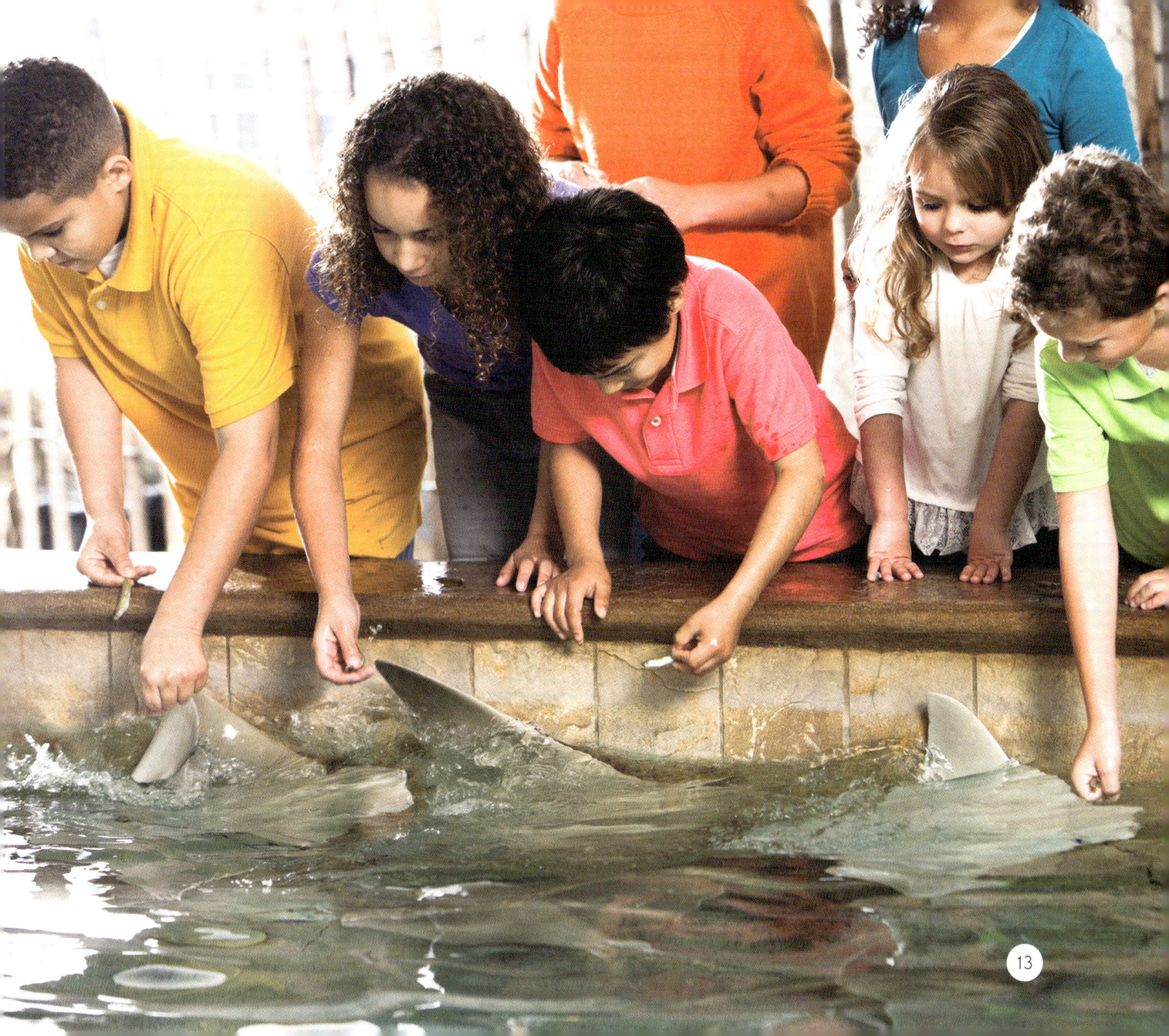

You look at lots of fish.

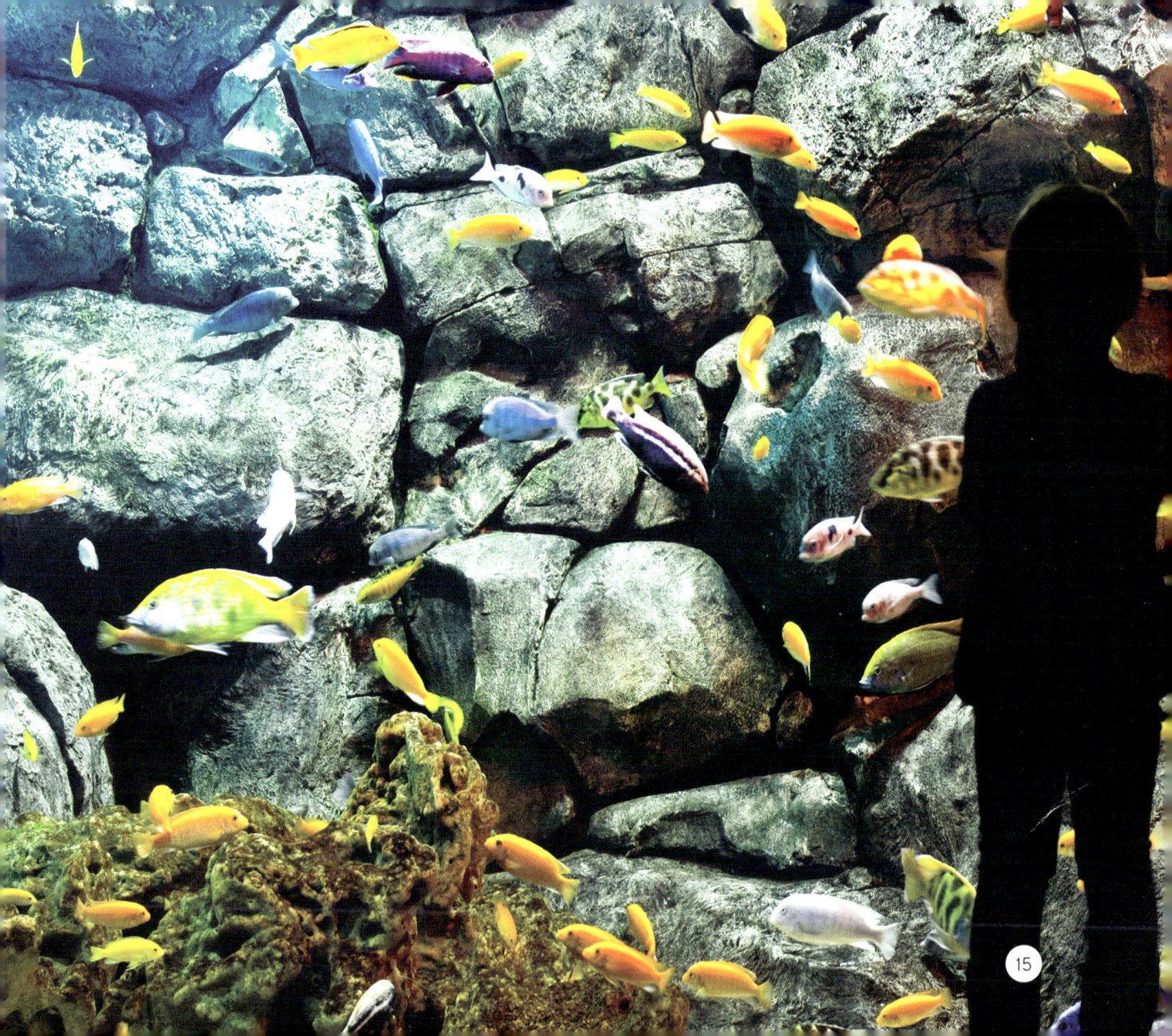

This fish looks at you!

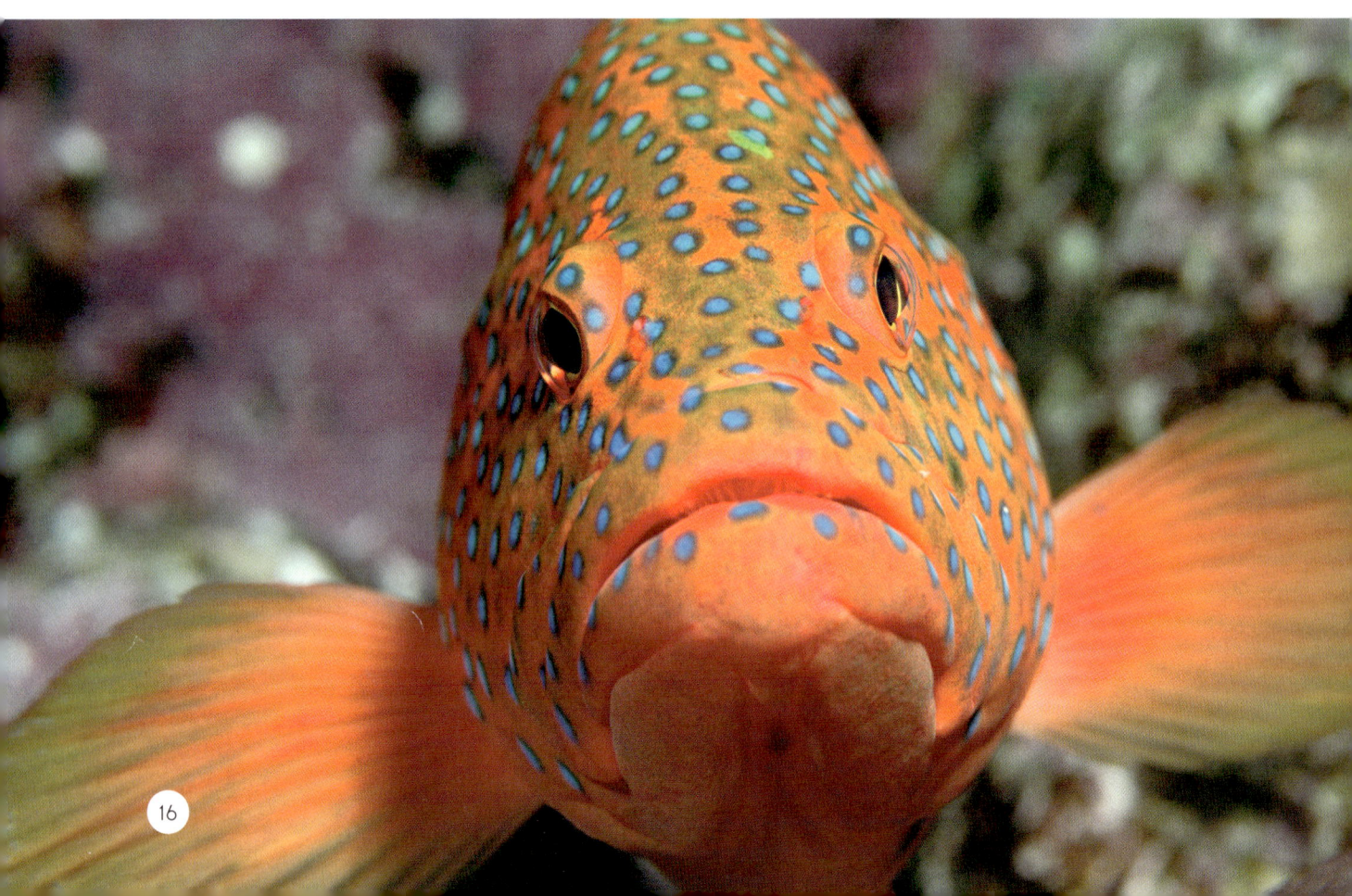